East-West Migration

East-West Migration

The Alternatives

Richard Layard
Olivier Blanchard
Rudiger Dornbusch
Paul Krugman

The MIT Press
Cambridge, Massachusetts
London, England

© 1992 The United Nations University

The World Institute for Development Economics Research (WIDER), based in Helsinki, Finland, is a research and training center of the United Nations University.

This book was set in Palatino by The MIT Press and was printed and bound in the United States of America.

Library of Congress Cataloging-in-Publication Data

East-West migration: the alternatives / Richard Layard... [et al.].
    p. cm.
  Includes bibliographical references.
  ISBN 0-262-12168-9
  1. Europe—Emigration and immigration—Economic aspects. 2. Free trade—Europe. 3. Capital movements—Europe. 4. Freedom of movement—Europe. 5. Europe—Politics and government—1989–
I. Layard, P. R. G. (P. Richard G.)
JV7590.Z8 1992
304.6'094—dc20
                                        92-24291
                                        CIP

Contents

Preface

The World Economy Group is an independent group of leading economists set up by WIDER to report on major economic issues. Last year they produced a widely acclaimed report on the general problems of economic transition entitled *Reform in Eastern Europe*. This year they comment on one of the huge problems that have been unleashed by these reforms.

This is the problem of migration. As the barriers between East and West have come down, so the pressure to move west has manifested itself. This poses the West a tremendous problem. For decades it preached about the inequities of penning people into their homelands. Now the East is willing to let them go, and the West is saying they cannot come. This raises major economic and social issues.

The authors put forward with great clarity the classic economic argument in favor of the free movement of labor. This is that, when people move in pursuit of higher wages, they are raising their own productivity. But the group also point to the social problems that migration can cause in both the receiving and the sending country. This leads them to examine other ways in which productivity can be raised without people moving.

There are two classic means. The first is trade. If trade barriers come down, workers in the East can produce for Western markets just as well as if they were working in the West. The group therefore argue strongly in favor of a European free trade area covering all countries East and West. But, as they point out, this will by no means eliminate the income gap between East and West. The migratory pressure will be only partially abated.

The other classic method for reducing income gaps between countries is the international flow of capital. Again the group point out that this can be only a smallish part of the total investment funds needed for economic development. But it can be a crucial part. If, like the Marshall Plan money, it has the right conditions attached, it can trigger good policies, which will do more to raise living standards than everything else put together. The group argue strongly for an imaginative aid package for the former Soviet republics, including a consolidation of the debt.

Do free trade and capital flows make migration unnecessary? The group do not think so. They argue that Europe should permit immigration of skilled workers on the same scale as the United States does. They show convincingly that this can do little if any harm to the existing Western workers. They have more anxiety about the impact of brain drain on the East. But to deny all hope of exit is to deprive the East of a vital safety valve and its citizens of a basic human right.

This is a stimulating report, full of information and penetrating economic analysis. I commend it to all the many policymakers concerned with the wide range of issues covered in the report.

Lal Jayawardena

Director of WIDER
Helsinki
9 December 1991

Acknowledgments

We are extremely grateful to the following for help with the data and arguments deployed in this book: George Borjas, Candido Cunha, Michael Emerson, Richard Freeman, Richard Jackman, Lawrence Katz, Vladimir Kosmarsky, John Murray, Stephen Nickell, Demetrios Papademetriou, Michael Piore, Leonid Rybakovsky, John Salt, Peter Schwansee, Alexander Shokhin, Guy Standing, Nina Tarasova, Myron Weiner, Holger Wolf, Hanya Zlotkin.

1   Overview

In West Berlin wages in dollars are ten times higher than in Poznan—less than 200 miles away. So a Polish worker can increase his income by a multiple of ten by a quite simple move.[1] Table 1 gives the comparable figures for other countries in Eastern Europe.

These disparities are not of course new. But there used to be a Berlin Wall. Since 1989 everything has changed. All Eastern European countries now let their citizens leave (and reenter) as they wish. The former Soviet Union is the sole exception, and there anyone will be able to leave from the beginning of 1993.[2]

Where income disparities are massive and movement becomes a possibility, the pressure to move is intense. And it will become much stronger as unemployment rises in the East. Until the income gap is reduced, the pressure to migrate will remain.

How much actual migration occurs will be governed by Ohm's Law, as in the flow of electric current. The flow will be proportional to the difference in income levels and inversely proportional to the resistance. So should the West resist?

Table 1
Wage gaps and populations, 1990

	Wage per hour (US $)	Population (millions)
Eastern Europe		
Poland	0.7	38
Hungary	0.7	11
Czechoslovakia	0.8	16
Bulgaria	0.2	9
Romania	0.6	23
Yugoslavia[1]	1.1	24
USSR (European)[2]	0.9	222
Eastern Europe (total)	0.9	343
Receiving countries		
Germany (West)	11	61
France	8	56
Italy	11	57
UK	8	57
EC (total)	9	340
EFTA (total)	13	25
Western Europe (total)	10	365
USA	13	250
Canada	13	27
Australia	14	17

Sources: Wages in Eastern Europe: Average monthly wages in local currencies for Poland, Hungary, Romania, Bulgaria, and Czechoslovakia taken from UN Economic Commission for Europe, *Economic Survey of Europe*, 1990–1991. Exchange rates from IMF, *Financial Statistics*. Hours worked per month taken from ILO, *Yearbook of Labour Statistics*, 1989–1990.

Wages in receiving countries: Average wage is taken from ILO, *Bulletin of Labour Statistics*, and updated by OECD, *Main Economic Indicators*, July 1991, p. 21, unless otherwise stated. Exchange rates from IMF, *Financial Statistics*.

Population: UN *World Population Prospects*, 1990.

1. Calculated from local currency wage quoted in ILO, *Yearbook of Labour Statistics* for 1988, and updated from OECD, *Quarterly Labour Force Statistics*, vol. 2, 1991, p. 168.

2. These figures are for Russia, the Baltic republics, Ukraine, and Belorussia. USSR average wage from *Houston Four*, vol. 2, p. 201, with the average weighted by employment from *Houston Four*, vol. 1, p. 230, table 31, converted at the commercial rate of Rs 1.8 = $1.

The Alternatives

In a world without controls, three main processes would operate that would eventually eliminate the income gap and thus the pressure to migrate.

1. Labor would flow to the West, where capital abounds.

2. Capital would flow to the East, where labor abounds.

3. Goods and services would be traded in both directions.

The first two processes would raise capital/labor ratios in the East toward those in the West, thus raising incomes in the East toward Western levels. Trade would also tend to equate capital/labor ratios in any given industry by letting the East export labor-intensive goods and import capital-intensive ones. This would tend to equalize real wages and rates of profit without the need for people to migrate westward or capital to move east.

So is the answer a total deregulation of the movement of labor, capital, and goods—as is the aim within the European Community?

There is an overwhelming case for complete freedom of trade, including agricultural as well as industrial products. But at the very least the European Community should offer the Eastern countries a free trade agreement like that being worked out between the United States and Mexico.[3] There is no special virtue in bringing Easterners to the West to produce labor-intensive goods, rather than enabling them to produce those goods at home and then sell them abroad.

Private capital flows are also a part of the solution. At present capital is biding its time, each investor wanting to be sure there are enough others, plus a prospect of political and economic stability. In this context a political lead is essential. Free trade is one key, since it enables Western investors to use cheap Eastern labor to capture Western markets. But clear property rights, free markets, and macroeconomic stability are also essential.

The East is poised between entry into a virtuous circle of economic reform and reconstruction and entry into a vicious circle of rising prices, leading to populist Latin American–style solutions and thus to further economic disaster. Sound economic policies will be extremely difficult to implement since they involve short-term pain. In this context external aid, conditional on good policies, can be a key catalyst. A major function of external aid is as a bribe to generate consensus in support of sound policies.

Most governments, including for example the British government in 1976, find it easier to administer a bitter pill if it is prescribed by a foreign doctor rather than by themselves. The same is true of most organizations—otherwise how could management consulting be such a flourishing industry? But the international management consultants based in Washington and Brussels need to bring real money with them to be convincing. Like Marshall Plan aid it will be tiny relative to domestic savings. But like Marshall aid it can make a big difference to the whole tenor of reform, and eventually restore the private capital flows that were moving before 1914. Debt relief will also help. But without new money, the international head teachers will find it difficult to influence their new disciples.

Reform in the East is in the interest of all, but above all of Western Europe, which will benefit from the new demand for its exports and from the diminished pressure to migrate. So Europe will have to pay a disproportionate amount.

But what else shall we do about the migration of labor? Should this too be unconstrained? It cannot be. For migration, though it benefits the migrant, can inflict external costs on those who live in the host country and in the country of origin. It has to be regulated if major social tensions are to be avoided. But by no means should it be forbidden. Freedom of movement is a basic element of human dignity, and this must include the prospect of being able eventually to migrate. The mingling of new people, though often painful, can bring new life to a nation, as has happened before with immigration from Eastern lands.

The concept of a "common European space" would be meaningless without permitting substantial permanent movement from East to West. The issue has to be not "Whether" but "How many?"

The Pressure to Migrate

One can hardly think about this without trying to estimate the likely pressure to migrate. There are currently about 3.3 million ethnic Germans in Poland, Romania, and the former Soviet Union.[4] Under the German constitution any German has the right to settle in Germany, and the majority of those in the East will probably move in the next decade.[5]

To form an idea of how many others would like to move, we can probably best look at the migrations from Southern Europe in the 1950s and 1960s and from Mexico in the 1970s and 1980s. Neither migration was uncontrolled (since most migrants were legal). But the numbers who actually moved provide some minimum estimate of the fraction of (non-German) people in the East who would want to move if they could. The estimate is probably a minimum because the costs of information and travel are constantly falling, and there is also the possibility of real economic and political disaster in the East.

Between 1950 and 1970 almost 3 percent of the population of Southern Europe shifted into Western and Northern Europe (5 million people), and a roughly equal number moved to the Americas. Since 1970, 4 percent of the population of Mexico has shifted into the United States. Are Europe and the United States together ready to accept say 3 percent of the population of the East? This would imply (in addition to say 3 million Germans) some 4 million others from the former Soviet satellites and 6 million from the European Soviet area— perhaps 1 million would-be immigrants a year.

If there were major ethnic conflicts or famine, the numbers could be much higher. If the worst happened, we should be talking about refugee camps and disaster relief. But we shall concentrate on the less dramatic scenario of say 1 million people a year wanting to move for many years to come.

Such migration has happened before. In the years before the First World War this was the rate of migration into the United States alone. But are we ready for it now?

The Response

Leaving aside refugees, the United States at present admits each year 160,000 primary migrants (without family ties in the United States). Europe admits virtually none. One response for Europe would be to persist in these policies. But this would be wrong. If people wish to move to better themselves, there is a strong presumption that they should be allowed to do so. Such moves generally increase world output.

There may of course be negative externalities: social tension and additional fiscal burdens imposed on others. And these can justify limits on those types of migration that impose such external costs. Clearly skilled workers are much less costly for the West to absorb, on both cultural and fiscal grounds. And there will be a high proportion of them willing to leave the East. We would therefore urge that Europe admit at least as many people as the United States currently admits on nonfamily grounds, and (like the United States) give preference to skilled workers. The United States should also increase its quota.

But, comes the reply, this will divest the East of just the workers that it needs in order to rebuild. The issue, however, is not so clear-cut. In the first place, emigrants invariably send home remittances that often exceed the whole of their income in the country they left. Such remittances are a major source of financial capital inflow (in Yugoslavia, Turkey, and Portu-

Millions

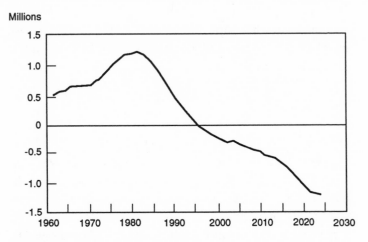

Figure 1
Net entrants to the Western labor force per annum, 1961 to 2025, assuming that
participation rates remain constant at the level of 1985. (Source: Eurostat,
referred to in Coleman, 1990.)

gal they finance a quarter or more of imports).[6] Moreover
emigrants rarely lose touch with their native land and often
return, acting as major conveyors of know-how.

Others will object that Western Europe just cannot absorb any
more bodies. Fortunately it does not have to. The growth of
the Western European labor force is nearly at an end (see
figure 1). There is a sharp decline in the number of young
people, which in some countries has already led to shortages
of young workers. More important, as time proceeds there
will be fewer and fewer people of working age to support each
elderly person or child. Thus there can be major fiscal advantages to the West from importing youngish, skilled workers
who can help to support the old, and will in due course be
supported by the fiscal contributions of their own children.

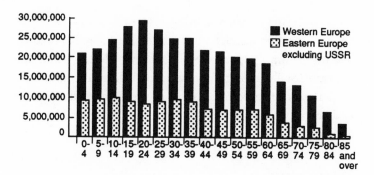

Figure 2
Population by age: Western and Eastern Europe, 1987. (Source: Coleman, 1990.)

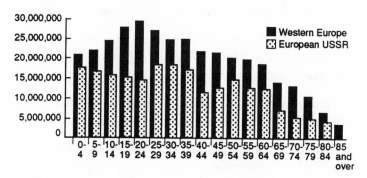

Figure 3
Population by age: Western Europe and European USSR, 1987. (Source: Coleman, 1990.)

This should be an important factor in the minds of Western voters when they consider the costs and benefits of immigration.

For the West it is therefore a happy coincidence that there are now a large number of young workers in the East (see figures 2 and 3). This is also relevant to the East, since some reduction in the large number of young adults may be no great loss during a period of rising unemployment there.

Thus we are in favor of migration but we recognize that it will have to be rationed. Such migration will act slowly in reducing the income gap between East and West, so that the pressure for illegal migration will remain. Illegal migration is an evil, since it produces a class of unassimilated migrants and hostility among nationals. It must be controlled by legal action.

Conclusions

But the best defense of all is economic progress. This requires urgent action in all the ways we have outlined.

1. *Trade.* The European Community should offer a free trade agreement, not on a country-by-country basis but as part of a pan-European free trade area.

2. *Capital flows.* The IMF and World Bank should persist with major aid packages conditional on radical economic reform.

3. *Migration.* A new Berlin Wall to keep people out would be as offensive as the old one that kept them in. The United States lets in 750,000 new residents a year, of whom 160,000 are primary migrants and their families. Western Europe, with a population greater than that of the United States, lets in almost no primary migrants and many fewer family migrants. Germany has to accept say 3 million ethnic Germans— perhaps the equivalent of the family migrants let in to the United States. But in addition the Community should surely accept as many primary migrants as the United States—a quota that could itself be raised.

2

Migration:
The Pressure to Move

The Setting

On 9 November 1989 the Berlin Wall was breached. The pressure to migrate was the cause, and the Eastern European revolution of 1989 the result. In the year that followed about 1 million people settled in West Germany, half of them from East Germany (*Übersiedler*) and half from Poland and elsewhere (*Aussiedler*).[1]

This mass migration of Germans has not yet run its course. On the basis of opinion polls Akerlof and his colleagues (1991) estimate that another half million East Germans are likely to move west. But more important are the 3.3 million ethnic Germans outside Germany, who have the constitutional right to reside in Germany. Allowing also for further movement from eastern to western *Länder*, it is likely that within a decade, West Germany will have to absorb up to 4 million extra Germans.[2]

However, ethnic Germans are only the tip of the iceberg of Easterners who will wish to migrate. To put a number on this,

we can begin by noting the populations of the Eastern countries and of the Western countries to which people might
migrate (see table 1). It seems likely that the non-Soviet people
of Eastern Europe will want to behave much like the peoples
of postwar Southern Europe or contemporary Mexico when
they find themselves in similar circumstances. In those situa-
tions we shall see that, starting from a position in which
movement had been very difficult, a situation developed
where within 30 years about 6 percent of the population had
moved to some richer country. If we focus on the next 15 years
and think in terms of 3 percent, this would imply that at least
4 million non-Soviet Eastern Europeans would wish to move
to Western Europe or the United States.

The former Soviet Union is more difficult to assess, since it has
always been more cut off, not least by its alphabet. But a
nationwide survey of 5,000 adults in March 1991 found that 4
percent would like to migrate permanently and a further 9
percent would like to work abroad for a considerable period.[3]
The 4 percent figure would imply some 12 million migrants,
which most Soviets regard as unrealistic. A figure often
quoted is the Union Ministry of Labor's estimate of 6 million.
This is in fact exactly 3 percent of the European population of
the USSR.

It must, however, be a quite conservative estimate. For the
Soviet space includes millions of ethnically displaced people.
Apart from 1.5 million Jews (most of whom will go to Israel or
the United States), there are 26 million Russians living outside
the Russian Republic. As these Russians suffer discrimination, they will begin to move. And once they move, many of

them will want to move West. Even those who would prefer to live in Russia may find no housing there. In many countries such Russians, fleeing discrimination, will be treated as refugees.

There are thus at least two possible scenarios for Eastern Europe.

1. Economic reform proceeds steadily. This involves some years of negative or low growth and growing unemployment. But within a few years recovery begins and growth is then good. Income levels, however, remain low and unemployment high, sustaining a strong pressure to migrate. Desired migration over 15 years might be of the order we have discussed—3 million Germans and 10 million others. This means a steady pressure of 1 million a year, roughly 0.3 percent of the population of Western Europe.

2. Things could be much worse if there is major civil strife in the former Soviet Union or elsewhere, or continued strife between Serbs and Croats. Almost every international border in the East is a matter of dispute, as are many borders between the former Soviet republics. This is the result of centuries of past migration. If it leads to present conflict, it could lead to further mass migration; we could see millions of refugees presenting themselves at the doors of Western Europe. Such refugees would be difficult to turn back, but in the extreme cases they would be put in camps (as in France during the Spanish Civil War) rather than admitted as regular migrants. There is also the possibility of famine in the Eastern countries, though this is much less likely. If it happened, this too would lead to refugee camps.

This is a broad-brush assessment. To give it more support, we can look briefly at the history of some earlier migrations and then at the econometric evidence about the determinants of migration.

Earlier Migrations

Ever since Abraham and before, people have moved to seek a better life. In the last four hundred years the biggest migration has been from Europe to the Americas. The population of the Americas is now nearly as large as that of Europe, and most families in the Americas are of European descent. Thus in a sense roughly half the population of Europe has moved to America.[4]

The rate of movement has of course varied. From the Irish Potato Famine until the First World War annual immigration fluctuated between 0.5 and 1.0 percent of the US population, with immigrants coming originally from Western and Northern Europe, and after 1870 mainly from Eastern and Southern Europe. The largest number of immigrants in any decade was the 8.8 million who arrived in the first decade of this century (see table 2). Of these, Jewish refugees were a very small proportion.

Until 1923 immigration was (except for Asians) unrestricted. But in 1923 Congress acted to prevent the continual dilution of Anglo-Saxon America. The number of visas was limited and made to reflect the ethnic make-up of the existing population. But after Hitler's war this ethnic basis for immigration seemed increasingly indefensible and was replaced by broadly the present system.

Table 2
Immigrants to the United States by decade

Decade	Number admitted (millions)	Admissions per annum as percent of total population	Foreign-born stock as percent of total population	Percent of immigrant flow coming from Europe
1820–1830	0.2	0.12		
1831–1840	0.6	0.39		
1841–1850	1.7	0.84		
1851–1860	2.6	0.93		
1861–1870	2.3	0.64		
1871–1880	5.8	1.29		
1881–1890	5.2	0.92		
1891–1900	3.7	0.53		
1901–1910	8.8	1.04	.14.2	
1911–1920	5.7	0.57	13.6	
1921–1930	4.1	0.35	12.1	
1931–1940	0.5	0.04	10.1	66
1941–1950	1.0	0.07	8.2	60
1951–1960	2.5	0.15	6.0	53
1961–1970	3.3	0.17	5.0	34
1971–1980	4.5	0.21	5.5	18
1981–1985	2.9	0.24	6.0	11
1820–1985	55.4	0.34		

Source: Borjas (1990), tables 1.1 and 2.2; Blackhurst (1991).

Under the current 1990 law the United States now admits as new permanent residents about 750,000 people a year. As table 3 shows, roughly two-thirds of these are relatives of US residents, 160,000 are regular primary migrants, and 120,000 are approved refugees. Eastern Europeans are likely to be major contenders for the places kept for nonfamily migrants.

There is also of course much illegal immigration into the United States, much of it across the land frontier with Mexico.

Table 3
Immigrants to the United States, 1992

Nuclear family members of US nationals (on demand)	218,000
Other relatives of US nationals and residents (quota)	281,000
subtotal	499,000
Worldwide lottery, to be replaced in 1994 by 55,000 places, allocated to countries in inverse proportion to their number of other immigrants (quota)	40,000
Skill (40,000 at each of 3 levels)	120,000
Refugees (quota)	120,000
Total	779,000

Source: US government estimates.

There are now probably some 3–4 million illegal immigrants in the country, of whom half are Mexican (Borjas, 1990). Although US employers are not allowed to recruit in Mexico, the number of Mexicans in the United States rose altogether by 3.2 million between 1970 and 1988—some 4 percent of the Mexican population.[5]

Within Europe, there have also been major movements of population. By 1914 both France and Germany had 1 million foreign residents, largely from the East. Between the wars France continued to take in foreigners, peaking at over 2.5 million foreign residents in 1931. But the Great Depression and the Second World War put a stop to migration.

After the Second World War and right up to 1961 there was a massive movement of Germans into West Germany. In the five years after the war 8 million Germans moved to West Germany from the East. And in the four subsequent decades 1950–1989, nearly 5½ million more moved, mostly in the years before 1961 when the Berlin Wall was erected to block their path.[6] France too had its own return, when in 1962 a million settlers came back from Algeria.

But more relevant to the future is the great movement of population out of Southern Europe in the 1950s and 1960s (see table 4). This was a period of high economic growth and low unemployment in Western and Northern Europe. Some of the migration was sponsored by employers but some by the workers themselves. German employers recruited in Yugoslavia and Turkey with the help of the German Federal Labor Institute. At the same time Italians (mainly from southern Italy) poured into Switzerland and further north, and Portuguese and Spaniards into France. The total net migration northward from these Mediterranean countries between 1950 and 1970 was about 5 million, or 3 percent of the total population of the Southern countries. In addition roughly equal numbers moved to the Americas (see table 5). Thus altogether about 6 percent moved abroad.

Table 4
Foreign nationals resident in Northern countries, in millions

Receiving country	1950	1970	1982
France	1.8	2.6	3.7
Germany	0.6	3.0	4.7
Benelux	0.5	1.0	1.5
Switzerland	0.3	1.0	1.0
Sweden	0.1	0.4	0.4
Total	3.3	8.0	11.3

Source: Maillat (1987), p. 40.
Note: We exclude Britain because it takes migrants mainly from the Third World and from Ireland (with which it was once united).

Table 5
Population living abroad as percent of total population (home and abroad), 1983

Country of origin	Percent in Europe	Percent in rest of world	Total abroad
Portugal	8.8	19.9	28.7
Spain	2.2	3.1	5.3
Italy	3.8	4.8	8.6
Yugoslavia	4.5	1.6	6.1
Turkey	4.3	0.6	4.9
All five countries	4.0	4.0	8.0

Source: OECD, *Employment Outlook*, September 1985, p. 54. Figures for 1983 or nearest year.

However, within Europe everything changed from 1974 onward. European unemployment rose, leading rapidly to a fall in the northward movement of population both between countries (see table 6) and within them (see figures 4 and 5). From 1974 onward all European countries stopped issuing further work permits to primary immigrants, though relatives continued to come in. The reason for the change of policy was partly unemployment and partly the pre-1974 buildup of communal tensions, which was then exacerbated by rising unemployment. Since 1974 the number of Southern Europeans (other than Turks) in the North has fallen. At the same time the number of North Africans in the North has continued to rise somewhat, and other North Africans have spilled over as illegal immigrants into Spain and Italy. There are now believed to be a half million illegal immigrants in Italy from a variety of countries (Calvaruso, 1987), and Spain too has become a country of net immigration.

Table 6
Southern nationals resident in Northern countries (France, Germany, Benelux, Switzerland, and Sweden), by country of origin, in millions

Country of origin	1970	1980	1985
Southern Europe			
Portugal	0.9	0.9	0.9
Spain	1.0	0.7	0.6
Italy	1.9	1.7	1.5
Yugoslavia	0.9	0.8	0.7
Greece	0.5	0.3	0.3
Turkey	1.2	1.8	1.8
North Africa			
Morocco	0.3	0.6	0.8
Algeria	0.7	0.8	0.8
Tunisia	0.1	0.2	0.2
Other	2.5	3.0	3.0
Total	10.0	10.8	10.6

Source: UN, *World Population Monitoring,* 1989, pp. 214–215. Definitions differ from those used in table 4.

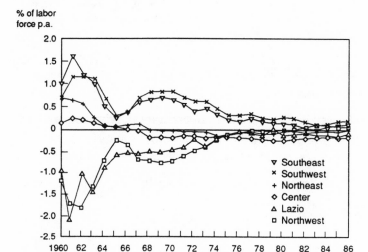

Figure 4
Net emigration in Italy, by region. Data concern migration between regions, expressed in percent of local labor force; migration abroad is excluded. (Source: Attanasio and Padoa-Schioppa, 1991.)

% of labor
force p.a.

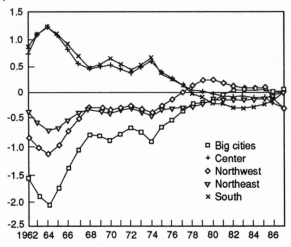

Figure 5
Net emigration in Spain, by region. Data concern migration between regions,
expressed in percent of local labor force; migration abroad is excluded. (Source:
Bentolila and Dolado, 1991.)

From this brief chronicle we can draw two provisional
conclusions.

1. Very large migrations can occur for purely economic reasons, despite large cultural and linguistic differences. They
tend to peter out, however, if jobs become hard to get.

2. Previous channels of migration help, but if employers want
labor new channels can develop rapidly. There were few
Yugoslavs and Turks in Germany in 1950.

What Determines Migration?

The next step is to look more closely at why people migrate
and to examine such econometric evidence as exists to see
whether it can help us forecast the likely demand to leave the

East. From our point of view what matters is of course the net flow of migrants. Many of those who leave eventually return, either because that was their original plan (Piore, 1979) or because they become disappointed, homesick, or bored. In fact even before the first World War the annual return from the United States equaled one third the annual inflow.

So what are the main factors affecting net migration? People do not automatically migrate when incomes are higher in one place than another, but their desire to migrate depends on: (1) comparative wage levels, actual and expected; (2) comparative unemployment rates and unemployment benefits; (3) the availability of housing; and (4) the costs of migration: travel costs (including availability of foreign exchange), information costs, and the psychic cost of leaving one's culture, friends, and relations. Thus both push and pull factors (that is, both internal and external conditions) matter. It is the comparison of conditions at home and abroad that determines behavior.

What evidence have we on how strongly the different factors operate in affecting the (net) desire to migrate? Unfortunately, international migration almost never reflects exactly the desire to migrate. In the twentieth century there have almost always been controls, and the strength of the controls has constantly varied, making econometric estimation virtually impossible.[7]

For internal migration within countries this problem does not arise, and there have been many studies that confirm the influences we have listed.[8] We survey some of these in appendix 1 and concentrate here on a few recent studies. We can begin with the findings of Barro and Sala-i-Martin (1991). Using panel data on US states, they find that, if a state has a per capita income 10 percent below the national average, it will experience a net emigration of 0.25 percent of its population per year, other things being equal.[9]

As the authors also point out, the process by which income differences get eliminated is slow. Between US states, about 2.5 percent of income differences are eliminated each year (in the absence of shocks). Interestingly, the same figure applies in Europe, both between countries and across regions within countries. This slow convergence explains why patterns of migration persist over a very long time.

The Barro and Sala-i-Martin analysis does not distinguish between the two main elements in income: the wage and the chances of getting a job. When this is done, the typical finding is that migration responds less to wages than to the chances of a job. For example, in Britain a 10 percent lower wage in a region increases its annual net emigration by 0.6 percent of its labor force.[10] But a fall of 10 percent in its employment rate raises annual net emigration by 0.8 percent of the labor force.[11] While migration depends positively on unemployment differentials, it is also often found to fall when the general level of unemployment is high.[12] This explains the remarkable fall in internal migration in Spain and Italy in the later 1970s (see figures 4 and 5).

What does all this tell us about the likely pressure to leave the East? If we took the Barro and Sala-i-Martin estimate and extrapolated it well beyond the range of sample values to a tenfold income difference, we should predict a desired annual emigration rate of nearly 6 percent of the population. The implications of other studies of internal migration would be similar.

But these numbers of course exceed the upper bound of any sensible guess. For leaving your country for a foreign land involves much higher psychic and financial costs than moving within a country. In addition, the information about jobs, housing, and travel may be much more limited for international moves.

Prospects for Desired Migration

So what *can* we say about the likely scale of desired migration? The wage gap is huge (see table 1). At present unemployment in the East is still rising. In Poland, which began its reforms first, unemployment is now over 10 percent of the nonfarm work force. It is most unlikely that the equilibrium unemployment rate in the East will be lower than the level of nearly 10 percent now found in Western Europe. And it seems highly likely that for some years in the 1990s Eastern unemployment will have to go above the long-run equilibrium level during the process of restructuring. This becomes even more likely if price liberalization generates ongoing inflation inertia that then needs to be squeezed out.

In fact, unemployment could be as important as wage gaps in generating pressure to leave. Akerlof and his colleagues asked a sample of East Germans about conditions in which they would migrate to West Germany, and found that a key determinant would be the availability of jobs in West and East.[13] This seems to portend continuing large-scale migration within Germany.

One important factor affecting unemployment is demographics. As figures 1–3 showed, the Western labor force will soon be shrinking, while the Eastern one expands. This reflects the fall in the Western birth rate since the mid 1960s (plus the retirement of large cohorts born before the Great Depression). The result is that in the West employers have begun to feel short of young labor, especially if it is well educated. This shortage varies between boom and slump, but Western employers may well become eager to employ well-educated Eastern European youth—just as in the 1950s and 1960s they hired Turks and Yugoslavs to make up for the shortage of youths caused by low wartime births.

At the same time in Eastern Europe large youth cohorts will be confronted with low demand for labor, caused by economic adjustment and recession. Many of them will surely seek their fortune abroad.

On top of this there is the prospect of major ethnic upheavals, which we have already discussed. Thus all the economic and political factors point to a major pressure to migrate. If we draw on the experience of migration from Southern Europe and from Mexico and add the element of unemployment and ethnic upheaval in the East, we should surely expect at least 3 percent to want to go west within the next 15 years.

Before Communism there was of course no comparable migration from the East. But travel and information were much more costly then, and more importantly the East was relatively rich. We now face a quite new situation, with massive pent-up demand to leave.

Time Pattern of Desired Migration

So how fast will this pent-up demand want to head west? The desired flow will persist for decades and decades. This may seem a surprising thought, but it is what we see in all cases where migration is unconstrained.

Why doesn't all the migration take place in a short period and then stop? One might think that there would be an equilibrium distribution of people between areas, in which the net advantages of different locations have been equated for the marginal worker. So why does the system not move to that equilibrium at once?

There are three main factors. The first is the limited rate at which receiving areas can absorb migrants. A rise in the migration rate puts pressure on housing and jobs, which chokes off some of the demand to migrate until the number of dwellings and jobs have adjusted upward. The second is the fact that most primary movers are young adults, and, as each new cohort comes along, so there is another pool of potential migrants. Third, information spreads over time. Each year, even in a country like Britain, new people hear of opportunities in other areas.

But, in the context of the East, there is a special issue to be considered: the backlog of unsatisfied migration. We are starting from a situation where virtually nobody could leave and where foreign currency was very scarce.[14] Once controls on migration are removed and foreign currency becomes easy of access, what would we expect to see? One approach would be a "stock adjustment" approach. The backlog would want to move very quickly, and the system would then fairly soon converge on a lower steady rate of leaving. This is illustrated in figure 6a.

There was clearly an element of this in the westward migration of 1989–1990 (though some of that migration was also motivated by doubts about the East, which may now have been somewhat alleviated). So should we conclude that future migration will be much slower than in 1990?

The "infection" model suggests the opposite. According to this, migrations build up over time, as information channels become established. On this basis, the rate of migration could first be expected to increase steadily, and then eventually tail off to a steady-state level as the backlog of those wishing to move is exhausted. This "infection" model would give a time path for the accumulated stock of migrants, as shown in figure 6b.[15]

Clearly there are important elements of truth in both these models. So perhaps the best guess is a combination of the two, shown in figure 6c. This suggests that, in the absence of shocks and major controls, desired migration per year will be fairly stable for some time, before eventually tailing off.[16]

This is in fact very much what happened in Southern Europe after the Second World War, as we have seen. Even as late as the early 1970s there were each year about 800,000 first-time immigrants to the North from Portugal, Spain, Italy, Yugoslavia, Greece, and Turkey.[17] But this was in the context of virtually no binding controls on immigration.

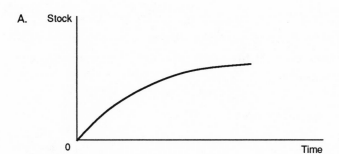

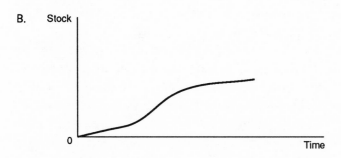

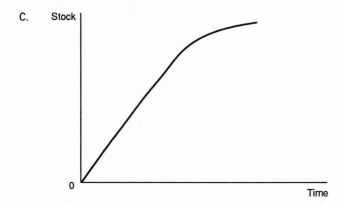

Figure 6
Building up the stock of workers living abroad.

This brings us (almost) to the key question of this book: Should immigration be controlled or even stopped? But before we tackle this, there remains one prior question: *Can* it be controlled?

Can Immigration Be Controlled?

The answer is that it depends on whether the authorities want to control it. If a country wishes, it can keep out most illegal foreigners, even across a land frontier. There are two main forms of control: at the border and inside the country.

Control at the border can have only limited effect, even when the country is an island. Provided tourism is allowed (and who would wish to stop it?), people are free to enter. They can of course be required to have visas, which can be conditional for example on adequate finance and a return air ticket. This is some deterrent since, even though the return ticket may not be used, the financial burden it imposes may put off some proportion of would-be one-way travelers. But most Western European countries have now abolished visas for Hungary, Czechoslovakia, and Poland. And, once into Europe, visitors will soon be able to travel freely among all eight countries that have abolished border controls through the Schengen Agreement (i.e., all European Community countries except Denmark, Greece, the United Kingdom, and Ireland).

Europe will still of course maintain its external border control in order to ensure that there is a proper record of all who enter, and Eastern visitors will have a clear expiry date by which they must leave or get a residence permit.[18] Thus Europe will discourage entry across fields or beaches. For this purpose Austria has already stationed its army on its border with Hungary, which was once guarded by Hungarian barbed wire to keep the people in. Likewise the United States operates a large border patrol along its endless border with Mexico.[19] In the 1980s, this caught about 1 million Mexicans a year who were trying an illegal entry without papers, but many got through.

Thus the main function of border controls is to establish the idea that foreigners can only enter a country for a limited time, unless they get a residence permit. But, for able-bodied adults, the most effective form of control is the work permit. In Europe work permits are normally given first for a particular job, but in due course, if extended, they become a general entitlement to work.

The real question therefore is whether the work permit system can be enforced. Clearly it cannot if the police connive with employers benefiting from immigrant labor. Much illegal immigration is public knowledge. For example in the Rue du Sentier (near the Paris Opera), hundreds of illegal Turks and South Asians are employed in the garment industry. But, even if the police act, the work permit system will not work unless there are real penalties on both employers and workers. In both Europe and the United States the fines on firms are relatively small (there are none in Britain, and fines in the United States began only in 1986).[20] For the worker himself the only penalty is generally that he is "taken to the frontier," not that he is prohibited from ever coming in on a legal basis. So why not take a chance?

In this situation it is not surprising that there is illegal immigrant labor in all countries. But its size is limited by the size of the black economy. An employer who is paying taxes for each worker will have to supply the worker's social security number. Unless the worker has managed to steal this, the employer will be in trouble. Large employers do not generally employ illegal immigrants—for this reason, and because they value their reputation.

The size of the black economy is limited both by the honesty of employers and by the potential size of the industries that lend themselves to black activity—construction, retail, repairs, cleaning, catering, and, above all, domestic service. In Britain the black economy covers about 3 percent of activity (Smith, 1986) and in Germany probably less. Mediterranean countries tend to have a different tax ethic and are more natural centers of illegal immigration.

The other main source of control over illegal immigration comes from the hazards of life. If you are involved in a car accident or a criminal investigation, or have to go to a hospital or send your child to school, people want to see your papers. In continental Europe, where everyone has to carry an identity card and register their place of residence, this is particularly embarrassing. It puts a real limit on the amount of illegal movement that is possible.

There is of course one standard way of bypassing the controls, which is to obtain refugee status. It is extremely difficult to know how many Eastern Europeans will qualify for this, since we cannot forecast the degree of ethnic strife. But under the

Geneva Convention everyone is entitled to *apply for* refugee status, and hearings take a long time to happen. By this time children are often in school and so on, and eventually many of those who apply for refugee status get accepted under some other rubric. Thus applying for refugee status is often in fact a good way to get accepted, even for nonrefugees. The refugee loophole has now become a major political issue and new restrictions are coming in.[21] But in any case the size of this loophole is probably smaller than the loophole of illegal immigration.

Neither loophole is desirable. Illegal immigration drives immigrants underground. It inhibits their efforts to assimilate and increases native resentment of immigrants. The real issue is how much legal migration we want. This depends on whether its effects are good or bad.

3   Migration: The Likely Effects

To think about this we need to begin with some basic theory and then see how it is borne out by the evidence. We must always distinguish between long-run effects and the short-run problems of adjustment when new workers arrive. In the long run we can probably assume that unemployment rates are independent of the size of the labor force—while the labor forces of Europe and the United States multiplied manyfold over the last hundred years, their unemployment rates displayed no clear trend. But in the short run, of course, a sudden rise in the labor force can easily cause problems, depending on whether these immigrants have skills that are in short supply. We can take the long-run question first and model simultaneously the causes and effects of migration.

Long-Run Effects

There will always be pressure to migrate from East to West so long as income levels are much higher in the West. If migration were allowed to proceed unfettered, it would go on until relative wages in the East had risen sufficiently.

Potential migrants also care about the unemployment rates in both places, and in making their comparisons will weight wages by some factor such as $(1 - \gamma u)$ where u is the unemployment rate and γ is probably higher than one (since immigrants tend to be taken last in the queue for jobs). Potential migrants will also care about other aspects of the quality of life, which people usually experience as superior in the places where they grew up and where they have friends and relatives. Thus we can say as a first approximation that migration will proceed up to the point where

$$W_W(1 - \gamma u_W) = W_E(1 - \gamma u_E)\phi$$

when W_W is wages in the West, W_E wages in the East, and ϕ reflects the nonpecuniary advantage of East over West for the marginal migrant. This is the famous Harris-Todaro (1970) condition.

Suppose ϕ were 3. Migration would cease when wages in the East had risen to roughly ⅓ their level in the West (compared with ¹⁄₁₀ today). How much migration would be needed from East to West? For simplicity we could assume that effective capital grows at the same rate in West and East and that unemployment rates are the same in West and East. Then, if we assume a Cobb-Douglas production function $Y = L^{\frac{3}{4}}K^{\frac{1}{4}}$, we reach the astonishing conclusion that almost all Eastern labor would have to move west. This is clearly an exaggeration,[1] but it underscores the scale of the pressure and the importance of knowing whether it should be accommodated or resisted.

Who gains and who loses from migration? For simplicity let us ignore unemployment. Then if only one person moved, he would gain $W_W - W_E \phi$. No one else would be significantly affected. So who could object?

But suppose lots of people move, so that in figure 7 the total labor force $(L_W + L_E)$ is distributed at the equilibrium point C, where net wages are equalized. In the initial distribution there were more people in the East, and lower net wages there. Who gains and loses in the transition?

In the West, the workers lose through the fall in wages, but the profit earners gain. *Altogether the West gains* by the triangle ABC. In the East, the remaining workers gain and the profit earners lose. *Altogether the East loses* by the triangle CDE. At the same time *the migrants gain* the rectangle ACED—though

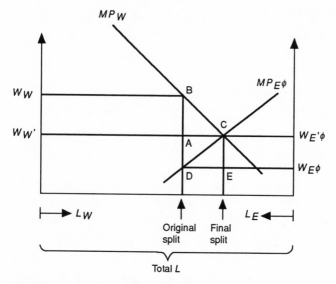

Figure 7
The effects of East-West migration.

they may well send home remittances that wholly or partly offset the loss to the East.

The world gains the Harberger triangle BCD. From the internationalist point of view this is the main result of migration. But from a national point of view it also matters who is gaining and losing, and this helps to explain the politics of migration. It explains why in receiving countries migration is favored by the rich and opposed by the poor, with the opposite true in sending countries.

But there are three important extra elements to consider. First, there are many types of labor. If we distinguish simply between skilled labor (S) and unskilled labor (N), we have a production function $Y = f(S,N,K)$. Immigration of any type of labor will make the existing workers of the same kind worse off, but this will be offset by gains to capital and to the other types of labor. Thus unskilled immigration may be quite popular among resident professionals. In the same way a brain drain from a country may be quite unpopular not only with its profit receivers but also with its unskilled workers, who fear for their public services and the leadership of their enterprises.

However, all this changes if we allow for capital mobility between countries. If the movement of workers into the West is accompanied by additional flows of capital, then Western capitalists will gain less and Western workers will lose less. Indeed the harmful effect on Western wages could be quite minimal. (There would be small losses to the types of labor heavily represented among migrants and small gains to other types of labor.) Equally, the Eastern countries would in this case get less capital than otherwise. Hence their workers' living standards would fail to benefit from the emigration.

Capital flows of this kind will only happen if existing rates of return are as high in the West as the East. Given the relative capital-abundance of the West one might not expect this to be the case, were it not for the low total-factor productivity in the East. Until this low productivity is remedied, it is quite likely that migration of labor from East to West would to an important degree divert capital to the West that would otherwise be invested in the East. And if capital moves when the migrants move, the migration has little effect on the average output of each nonmigrant worker in the East or West. But the migrant workers gain and so does world output. There is a pure efficiency improvement with few distributional consequences.

Externality Issues

In the analysis we have presented so far, whatever happens is best, at least in efficiency terms. But this isn't necessarily realistic, for many reasons.

1. *Wage compression.* Wages may not correspond to marginal productivity. In the East the wage structure is much more compressed than in the West. This makes skilled people particularly keen to move,[2] and indeed provides them with an excessive incentive to do so, since the gain to world output when they move is less than their own private gain. The difference here corresponds to an additional cost to the East when they move. This problem would not arise if the wage distribution in the East were corrected.

2. *Fiscal externalities.* Another source of externality is the tax transfer system. When a person migrates to the West, Western taxpayers receive the net taxes (taxes minus public expenditure) paid by the migrant. Eastern taxpayers lose the net taxes he paid in the East. The size of these net taxes varies of course between different types of migrant. The average migrant from Eastern Europe will probably earn in the West less than the average wage, while in the East he earned more than the average wage. Thus, when he moves, he may impose net costs on others in both the West and the East, making unrestricted migration excessive.

Of course if the migrant had a job and came on his own, without dependents, he would pay substantial net taxes. If immigrants are young and skilled there can be major fiscal gains to local residents. But historical experience shows that, though many migrants come on their own, intending to return, the majority of migrants who stay eventually bring their families. The dependency ratio in the foreign-born population of Western Europe has since the 1960s been very close to the average (Maillat, 1987, p. 52). It is therefore wrong to base immigration policy too heavily on the hoped-for fiscal exploitation of the lone migrant wage earner. Even the lone worker is liable to unemployment. In 1983 the unemployment rates of foreign workers in Belgium, France, Germany, Sweden, and Switzerland were between 50 and 100 percent higher than for nationals (Maillat, 1987, p. 53). In general unemployed foreigners in Europe receive the same unemployment benefits as locals.

Thus a key issue from the point of view of the receiving country is the skill level of the migrant. Skilled migrants will benefit the residents of the West through fiscal transfers.

They will also of course impose more damage on those who remain in the East. The fiscal aspect of brain drain has a further wrinkle, however. For skilled workers not only pay higher taxes but they have already received an expensive education at public cost. If such workers stay at home, they partly repay in taxes the public cost of their education. But if they leave, this cost is never repaid. Once migration has become an established option for educated people, more people will want to become educated. As before, higher education will attract as many people as can get an adequate yield on their education by staying at home, plus the extra number flowing abroad. This can be a major public expenditure with no offset in future tax yields.

This has led Bhagwati (1976) and others to propose a brain drain tax. According to this, migrants to the West would pay an extra education-related tax in the West that would then be passed back to the government in the East. There are, however, major difficulties with the proposal. First, there is the problem of measuring the relevant cost of education. Second, Western electorates would not like their governments to compensate Eastern governments rather than themselves for the consequences of the migration process (though this could be dealt with by making the migrants reimburse their countries directly). But the largest objection is a political one: the control and supervision needed to implement the proposal would inevitably set further red tape in the way of the free movement of labor.

3. *Cultural externalities.* The reason for the political reaction to migration is, of course, xenophobia. Most people in most countries find foreigners disturbing. The problems get worse (in ascending order) if (1) the foreigners or their children have

language difficulties, (2) they have different religious customs, or (3) they are black. Eastern Europeans are thus much less problematical than North Africans. But, when we see the intolerance of West Germans for East Germans, we should expect substantial problems with other Eastern Europeans who do not even speak German.

There may also be a negative externality in the sending country. When people migrate, they may leave their relatives and friends bereft. The migrants may of course have taken this into account. But more educated migrants (especially) often have important, unpaid, social positions that could be difficult to fill. Against this there is the important function of migration as a social safety valve, relieving tensions that might otherwise explode on the streets of the sending country.

4. *Market size effects.* A further problem arises if market size of itself increases the efficiency of production. For as people leave the East, its market size declines. Production in the East for the East then becomes less economic at existing wages, as there are fewer units of output over which to spread the fixed costs. More production then transfers to the West—reducing labor demand in the East, increasing it in the West, and inducing further migration (if migration is unrestricted). In the presence of increasing returns there may well be multiple equilibria, and given the distortions we have already mentioned, there is no presumption that the equilibrium with massive migration is superior to the equilibrium without migration (Krugman, 1991). This is a serious issue, especially in relation to skilled labor. If too many bright people leave before growth resumes in the East, its long-term future is imperiled. We discuss the formal issue more fully in appendix 2 and conclude that, while it is important, it should not be exaggerated.

5. *Information and endogenous tastes.* Most of the externalities discussed so far are negative and suggest the danger of too much unrestricted migration. But there are two points of an opposite kind. Potential migrants are ill informed about how they would fare in the West. Such information is a public good, and it may well be underprovided. In addition, movement itself leads to the transmission of know-how around the world, in a way that benefits many more than those who move (especially people in the country of origin).

There is also the problem of endogenous tastes. People generally like the place where they grew up. This makes adults loath to leave, and tends to freeze the distribution of peoples across the globe. But this reflects the tastes of adults. It takes little account of the fact that, once the adult has moved, his children will be born in the new country—and regard this as home. Thus it is quite possible that, if we took into account the welfare of future generations directly (rather than through parents' preferences), we should favor a much higher level of international migration than parents would choose without additional inducements.

6. *Conclusion so far.* So we cannot be sure whether migration, if unrestricted, would be more or less than optimal. But in fact migration is likely to be highly restricted. This brings into play a further argument. The freedom of the individual to move between countries is an important value in itself. In Europe it is a central feature of the European Community, and the wish of Europeans to inhabit a "common European space" recognizes this value on a wider scale. Freedom of movement is a good because it reduces individual frustration.

Western Europe should, if possible, be as open as the United States to people from outside. The United States, with a smaller population than Western Europe, admits 750,000 people a year. But we recognize that Western Europe will not do this. The most that can be hoped for is equality in the numbers of primary migrants.

But this leaves open the question of what kind of migrant should be encouraged. The argument differs according to whether one adopts the perspective of the East or the West. The West would prefer the more skilled migrants, the East would probably prefer the less skilled. But since it is the West that calls the tune, and will be holding migration below its optimal level, it is natural to give particular weight to Western preferences.[3]

A further argument for favoring skilled migrants comes from a totally different consideration. This is the problem of short-run adjustment.

Short-Run Absorption

In grappling with this problem, we shall begin by disregarding questions of the skill mix. In the very short run the real wage in the West is fixed and so therefore is employment. The same may be true in the East. So an exogenous increase in migration simply shifts unemployment from the East to the West. This is so even if migrants are required to have jobs, since to get the jobs they must have displaced other workers.

But, as unemployment rises in the West, this puts downward pressure on wages, and in due course Western unemployment will revert to its original level. If the migration is large this can take some time, as there may be some physical capital constraint that limits employment, as in postwar Germany.

With today's greater capital mobility, this adjustment would not take as long as it did then. In addition, the greater integration of world product markets will make it easier to sell at once the extra potential output.

But massive immigration on the immediate postwar scale is in any case unlikely. In the face of say an extra ¼ percent a year growth in population (the equivalent of 1 million immigrants a year), the process of adjustment could be quite fast. For the main mechanism of hysteresis in unemployment is the buildup of a group of demoralized and benefit-dependent long-term unemployed.[4] If, instead, the unemployed include a dispro-portionate number of people who have come to the West to find work, they may be more efficient job seekers than the native unemployed. This will cause the increase in unem-ployment not to persist so long. One is indeed struck by the failure of unemployment to rise in West Germany in 1990–1991, despite massive immigration.

We have so far discussed the effect of an exogenous migration. In the disaster scenario, which is one of the possibilities, there would of course be exogenous migration to the West. But the more likely development over the next decade is waves of migration, fluctuating with conditions in the West as well as in the East. This is how migration usually fluctuates (Thomas, 1954, 1972). If the migrants come during Western booms, they could actually stabilize the fluctuations in the unemployment rate rather than amplify them.

We can turn now to the issue of skill. The natural rate of unemployment in the West depends on the degree to which the pattern of labor supply is consistent with the pattern of

labor demand at current relative wages.[5] Suppose there are
some higher-level skills whose share in labor demand exceeds
their share in labor supply, and other lower skills where the
reverse applies. Then the natural rate of unemployment will
be higher than it would be if there was a better balance
between the pattern of labor demand and supply. Thus if
migrants are disproportionately endowed with skills in short
supply, migration could actually lower the equilibrium unemployment rate, with consequent fiscal externalities. As
Hansen (1991) points out, this argues strongly in favor of
permitting immigration mainly when it is sponsored by
employers, and allowing work permits to be given mainly for
actual jobs that have been offered—rather than for the right to
seek work.

Similarly emigration is on balance likely to reduce unemployment in the sending country. Those who leave will tend
to be those with the highest unemployment rates.

We can now look at the evidence of the effects of immigration
in some key recent migrations. We begin with the United
States and then look at France after the Algerian settlers
returned and at Germany after the massive immigration of
1945–1950. Further evidence is given in appendix 1.

Effects in the United States

The United States has been admitting roughly a half million
immigrants a year over the last two decades, increasing its
population by roughly 0.2 percent a year. This is a fairly gentle
immigration, though in some cities its impact is fairly spec-
tacular—in New York, Los Angeles, and Miami, 6–8 percent

of the population in 1985 had immigrated to the United States in the last five years (Butcher and Card, 1991).

Research on the effects of this migration has mainly compared cities and focused on changes in the proportions of foreign immigrants, and the associated changes in wages (and unemployment). The best of these studies is by Altonji and Card (1991), and relates to the 1970s. They found that, when the number of immigrants in a city increased by 1 percent of the labor force, native wages fell by around 1.2 percent. This finding is quite striking given that in the 1970s natives tended to move out when immigrants moved in, thus mitigating the effect of immigrants upon the total labor force (Filer, 1992).[6] While many US studies have claimed to find no effects of immigration on native wages, this does not seem to be true of the best studies.[7]

One obvious point is that cross-sectional results cannot easily be translated into inferences about aggregate national effects. If immigrant labor arrives somewhere and natives leave, there may be no relative wage effect where the migration occurs. But at the national level real wages will fall, unless international capital flows alter in response to the movement of labor.

These difficulties have led some writers to estimate the aggregate impact of immigration in an indirect rather than a direct manner (Borjas, Freeman, and Katz, 1992). Between 1980 and 1988 immigration raised substantially the fraction of the US labor force that had completed less than a high school education (see table 7). Thus in 1988 the fraction of less-educated workers was 7 percent higher than it would have

Table 7
Fraction of US labor force with less than completed high school education

	1980	1988
A Excluding immigrants	20.8%	13.4%
B Including immigrants	22.0%	15.2%
B/A	1.058	1.134

Source: Borjas, Freeman, and Katz (1992).

been if in each skill group the ratio of immigrants to natives had been the same as it was eight years earlier. To estimate the effect of this change upon the US wage structure, the authors use an aggregate time-series regression.[8] This shows that the relative wages of the less-educated fall by just over 0.3 percent when their relative numbers rise by 1 percent. On this basis immigration between 1980 and 1988 cut the relative earnings of less-educated Americans by 2.5 percent.

Analyses of this type are useful in showing how the distributional effect of immigration depends crucially on the mix of skills among immigrants. Under any likely policy for Eastern European immigration, the skill distribution of the immigrants would be at least as favorable as that of the natives. So migration would be unlikely to widen the wage differential among natives.

The Return of the French Algerians

In Europe the most dramatic migration between 1950 and 1989 followed the French agreement in March 1962 to give independence to Algeria. Within a year, 900,000 people of European origin (*pieds noirs*) returned to France—with skills on average rather above those among the existing French population. The event was highly exogenous and the choice of where to settle in France was relatively exogenous: the majority chose the sunniest parts of France. In 1968 there were 330,000 repatriated workers from Algeria, constituting 1.6 percent of the French labor force.

In terms of reemployment the repatriates seem to have fared relatively well. Their unemployment rate peaked at 20 percent in December 1962 but fell to 6 percent within the following year and 4 percent a year after that (Hunt, 1991, fig. 4b). In 1968, 4.5 percent were unemployed, compared with 2.1 percent of the whole French labor force.

How did the migrants affect existing workers? To assess this, Hunt (1991) compared the change in wages and unemployment between early 1962 and 1968 in different departments, according to the proportion of repatriates in the work force in 1968. Where repatriates constituted an extra 1 percent of the work force, the unemployment rate of natives was roughly 0.2 points higher. The effect on average annual earnings was less clear, but may have been of the order of 0.7 percent. There was no evidence of natives moving out where immigrants moved in, so that these results may give a reasonable measure of aggregate effects.

Postwar Germany

A much greater challenge was that faced by Germany in the immediate postwar period. Between 1945 and 1950, 8 million Germans moved into West Germany; another 4 million followed in the period from 1950 until 1961, when the Berlin

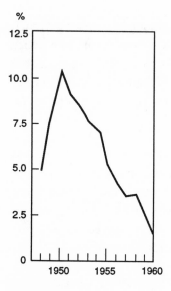

Figure 8
Unemployment rate in West Germany, 1948–1960. (Source: Giersch, Paqué, and Schmieding, 1991.)

Wall was built. This huge influx was extremely difficult to handle. One might suppose that the problem would have been worst just after the war, when much of the nation's capital could not be fully operated due to war damage. But during that period many of the refugees went to the countryside, where their unemployment was hidden rather than open. As the economy began to recover after the 1948 price liberalization and currency reform, open unemployment soared (see figure 8). Peak unemployment was reached in 1950. In 1951 the economy once again expanded fiercely due to the Korean War boom. Unemployment fell slowly but steadily throughout the miraculous years of the 1950s, and by

1960 unemployment had virtually disappeared. The immigrants, from being a liability, had become a major engine of growth—employed through a huge surge of capital investment (Kindleberger, 1967).

The lesson of this episode seems to be that huge numbers of immigrants can be absorbed in a well-functioning economy, provided they are socially acceptable. But if the flow is very high, transitional unemployment is unavoidable.

Can the West Cope?

What conclusions follow for our present predicament? No one is proposing an inflow remotely approaching the invasion that descended on West Germany after the war. If Western Europe admitted, say, 300,000 people a year as primary immigrants or refugees, this would be about 0.1 percent of its population.

This is less than one-third the typical rate of immigration into the United States. Some people will consider the comparison with the United States irrelevant on the grounds that the US has more land. But history shows that in modern economies natural resources and land are in no way essential for nations to prosper.

The real issue is the one of short-run adjustment. Migration equal to 0.1 percent of population should be quite manageable. But it is essential that the numbers be controlled. They could cause genuine unemployment if they are allowed to surge, especially at times of economic recession. And, if that happens, they will be a major source of social tension. But controlled admission to the West of well-educated fellow Europeans ought not to be a source of tension. It can only be achieved in a nonracist way by an immigration policy based on skill, and it needs to be accompanied by strong measures to control illegal immigration. It would be shameful to reerect the Berlin Wall. We can do better.

4   Free Trade
with the West

Given the difficulties posed by the prospect of very large-scale migration from East to West, and the risk that such large-scale migration could actually leave the remaining population in the East worse off, we need to ask what alternatives are available. Ideally, policy should try to bring good jobs to the East rather than Eastern workers to the West. International trade and investment *can* act as substitutes for migration. A free trade pact that ensures Eastern European countries access to the Western European market is the best single migration policy that could be put in place. In the amazing postwar reconstruction of Western Europe, the openness of the US market was a crucial factor. Western Europe now has the opportunity to provide a similar service to the East.

It is important, however, to be realistic about what such a pact could accomplish. Free trade will probably help reduce the incentives for migration, but it will certainly not be enough to eliminate these incentives.

Prospects for Growth in Trade

A first question is how much East-West trade to expect if Eastern European nations gain free access to Western markets. While any such estimates are tentative, it is possible to make some fairly good back-of-the-envelope guesses. The pre-1989 situation of Eastern Europe was straightforward. Individually the Eastern European nations were quite open to international trade, essentially to the same degree as Western nations. The direction of their trade was, however, biased away from the West and toward one another. Thus collectively Eastern Europe plus the Soviet Union formed a highly protected, closed economy. With the old regimes gone, their trade will now shift toward its "natural" direction.

The old pattern of trade is already eroding rapidly, and the outlines of the natural pattern of trade can already be seen. In Western Europe, trade as a share of GNP is strongly related to population while showing little correlation with per capita GNP. In time Eastern Europe should show a similar relationship. Thus despite the great uncertainty about the likely future levels of income in the new market economies, we can predict the share of trade in GNP with reasonable confidence. Hungary, for example, will probably trade about as much as Austria; Poland as much as Spain. Overall, then, Eastern European nations will probably export 25–30 percent of their GNP. The direction of the trade is also fairly clear: the sheer logic of purchasing power—the gravitational pull of the nearby Western European market—implies that Eastern European nations will do most of their trade with the European Community. This sort of logic allows us to predict that, with free market access, East-West trade will be some 20–25

Table 8
Trade of non-Soviet Eastern Europe with EC, as percent of Eastern European GNP

	Actual 1988	Predicted
Exports	3.2	11.4
Imports	3.1	10.8

Source: Collins and Rodrik (1991).

percent of Eastern Europe's GNP, an increase of 15–20 percentage points over pre-1989 levels.

It is possible to try to be more detailed than this, by using gravity models or other methods to attempt to predict the detailed pattern of trade. In a recent study by Collins and Rodrik (1991), pre-1929 trade flows are used as a shortcut way of measuring "natural" patterns of trade; this does surprisingly well at predicting the direction of trade for existing market economies. When the method is applied to the Eastern European nations, it produces a set of predicted trade flows; the resulting forecasts are shown in table 8. The general order of magnitude of the predicted flows is in the same range as our back-of-the-envelope numbers.

The important question, however, is the *significance* of the potential trade flows for the Eastern European countries.

Trade as a Substitute for Migration

In orthodox models of international trade, both trade and international factor mobility are driven by differences in factor proportions between nations. Thus nations with a high ratio of capital to labor tend to export capital-intensive goods,

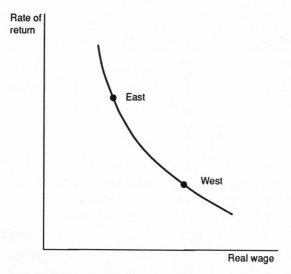

Figure 9
The factor-price frontier.

import labor-intensive goods, invest abroad, and be the target of emigration. Greater trade in goods can reduce the incentives for trade in factors. Indeed, in the limit trade can in principle lead to the exact equalization of factor prices across countries.

The logic behind this standard proposition may be illustrated by thinking of the tradeoff between the earnings of capital and labor, illustrated in figure 9. The curve illustrates the tradeoff between the real wage rate and the rate of return on capital. In the simplest case, we think of Eastern and Western Europe as sharing a common technology, and hence the same tradeoff, but of the East as being short of capital. As a result, capital is expensive in the East and the real wage rate is low.

Evidently this situation creates an incentive for emigration from East to West. It appears also to create an incentive for Western capitalists to invest in the East. We will discuss shortly why this incentive may be less strong than it might first appear to be, and in the next section why the prospects for investment are further limited by political and economic uncertainty. Meanwhile, however, we note that there is a third way of narrowing the wage gap, namely international trade. By exporting labor-intensive goods and importing capital-intensive goods, the East can in effect export labor embodied in its exports and import capital embodied in its imports. The net effect will be much as if the capital and labor had moved directly.

To what extent can this kind of indirect trade in factors substitute for actual migration? In the last chapter we argued that a huge fraction of the Eastern labor force would have to move for wage differentials to narrow to 3:1. If our previous suggestive calculations on trade flows are of the right order of magnitude, they will fall far short of these kinds of effect.

Suppose, for example, that an Eastern country is able to export to the West goods in which unskilled labor accounts for 70 percent of value added, and to import goods in which it accounts for only 30 percent. Suppose also that the country is able to export 20 percent of GNP to the West. Even so, the effect will be equivalent only to the out-migration of 8 percent of the labor force[1]—not insignificant, but not enough to move equilibrium wages anywhere close to Western levels. (If wages are stuck at a disequilibrium level, however, trade could make a substantial difference to unemployment, and thus help stem the pressures for migration.)

In any case, however, figure 9 represents an oversimplification of the situation. Unfortunately, the wage differential between Eastern and Western Europe is not simply a matter of scarce capital but also one of differences in economic efficiency. This considerably alters the story.

Efficiency Differences and Factor Mobility

While capital—particularly appropriate capital—is scarce in Eastern Europe, scarcity of capital is not the only explanation of low productivity. Instead, much of the blame must rest on the Communist legacy of distorted incentives, bad management, and low morale. While it is to be hoped that over time the Eastern European countries will be able to overcome their institutional problems, for the time being (and for the foreseeable future) the picture looks like figure 10 rather than figure 9:

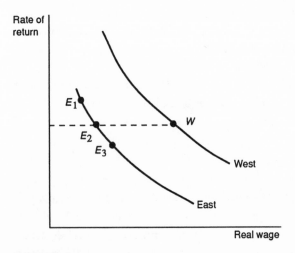

Figure 10
Two different factor-price frontiers.

the East operates on a worse tradeoff than the West as well as having scarcer capital.

As long as the underlying tradeoff is worse in the East, trade cannot be a full subsitute for migration. It can mitigate the effects of capital scarcity on the Eastern European wage rate, but it cannot fully eliminate the wage gap.

Perhaps even more important, the persistence of efficiency differences makes it questionable whether investment flows can be much of a substitute for migration either. Suppose, for example, that the initial position of Western Europe is at point W in figure 10, while that in Eastern Europe is at E_1. Capital flows from West to East will lower the rate of return in the East and raise the wage rate. (They will do the reverse in the West, but this much smaller effect is disregarded for simplicity.) They will not, however, equalize the wage rate; even if enough capital flows east to equalize the rate of return, the process will stop at E_2, with the Eastern European wage rate still considerably lower than in the West.

Indeed, it is by no means certain that capital will flow in the right direction. Although capital is scarcer in Eastern than in Western Europe, and is therefore relatively more expensive as compared with labor, it is possible that Eastern European efficiency is so much lower than that in the West that the initial situation is at a point like E_3, where the rate of return on investment is actually less in the East. In this case we would expect to find capital flowing not into capital-starved Eastern Europe but out to the more prosperous West.

We regard this situation as unlikely; but it serves as a stark reminder that neither trade nor investment will do much to remedy Eastern Europe's economic difficulties unless there is also an improvement in the overall efficiency of the Eastern European economy.

The main argument for a free trade pact is the hope that it will do exactly that: that East-West trade will be more than an indirect exchange of factors, but will instead become a force for greater efficiency in the Eastern European economies. We turn now to that aspect.

Dynamic and Macroeconomic Gains from Trade

Since the 1960s it has become increasingly clear that outward-oriented developing countries (those that have relatively liberal trade regimes or that offset the antiexport bias of tariffs with export promotion policies) tend to grow noticeably faster than nations following inward-looking, import substitution policies. The difference in growth rates tends to be several percentage points per year, which implies over time a cumulative dynamic benefit from outward-oriented policies that is much larger than conventional estimates of the static benefits from removing protection.

The sources of the dynamic gains from trade are a matter of considerable uncertainty. They certainly involve, however, the effects of trade in promoting competition and the opportunity to exploit economies of scale, among other factors. Aside from the former Soviet Union, all of the Eastern European nations have tiny domestic markets by comparison with the

European Community. Indeed, as a group the non-Soviet Eastern nations probably have a combined GNP not much more than 10 percent that of the EC. Thus, if they are allowed to become part of the unified European market, they will be in a position to shift their wage-profit tradeoff out substantially.

It is also likely that a free trade agreement between East and West would induce substantial direct investment into Eastern nations. Such direct investment, in addition to bringing capital, can serve as a valuable conduit for knowledge—both technology per se and, even more important, the know-how needed to operate in a market environment. In peripheral nations in Western Europe such as Portugal, direct investment aimed largely at export production has become an important engine of growth. It is reasonable to hope that the same can happen in the East.

The dynamic gains from increased trade with the West, perhaps reinforced by direct foreign investment that is also attracted in part by export opportunities, represent the real reason for hoping that access to Western markets will in the long run prove an alternative to migration.

There may also be shorter-run macroeconomic benefits from trade opening. It appears that highly open economies, having in effect given more hostages to the international financial market, are regarded as better risks (other things being equal) than more closed economies, and are therefore less likely to be cut off from credit when faced with adverse shocks. The experience of the 1980s has been that outward-looking developing economies have been far more successful at avoiding economic crisis, and in particular deep recessions induced by foreign exchange shortage, than those whose industry is largely oriented toward the domestic market. In particular, East and Southeast Asian countries, many of which exported more than 30 percent of gross domestic product as early as 1980, weathered the storms of the 1980s much better than inward-looking countries in Latin America.

In the context of migration, this is particularly important. As noted in chapter 2, the evidence on determinants of migration strongly suggests that availability of employment is more important than the wage rate as a determinant of migration. To the extent that Eastern Europe is successful in its *macroeconomic* performance—even if it takes decades for wages to converge to Western European levels—there may be only limited pressure to migrate.

Prospects

Neither access to the Western European market nor availability of Western capital are panaceas for the economic problems of Eastern Europe. In particular, the idea that trade and/or investment can fully substitute for migration are based on a far too simplistic model of the income disparity: large and probably persistent efficiency differences will limit investment prospects and provide a continuing incentive to migrate for a long time to come.

Nonetheless, a free trade agreement between East and West will be a major aid to the Eastern economies, and will thus help mitigate, though not eliminate, the pressure to migrate.

If bilateral negotiations of each country with the European Economic Community prove too cumbersome, a new organization may be needed to develop free trade arrangements within the whole European economic space.

Aid and Capital Flows

Thus trade and labor migration can do something to raise living standards in the East. But the most important factor will be the modernization of production in the East. This is partly a matter of organization (free markets and private ownership). But there is also a massive need for new capital in factories, offices, communications, hospitals—everywhere. How is this to happen, and what is the role of external finance?

Necessary Conditions for Investment

The amount of investment will be totally inadequate unless the conditions are right. That is the key point. It applies equally to investment financed at home and financed from abroad.

Under a command economy it was possible, at least for a time, to have satisfactory investment rates through centralized command. But once centralized command goes, investment withers unless proper market incentives replace the old command system.

At least three conditions are essential, as Latin American experience testifies.

1. Property rights must be clear. Without clear property rights no one knows who will get the return on investment, and investment demand dries up. Vesting property rights in a clearly defined public institution (so-called commercialization) can only partly serve this purpose, since most people know that the next step will be privatization. Rapid privatization is the best guarantee of a recovery of investment (Blanchard and Layard, 1991).

Clear property rights (including the right to repatriate profits) are even more crucial in securing a flow of foreign private capital. Where property rights are in question, as in Venezuela and Brazil, price/earnings ratios run amok. As Luigi Einaudi, Italy's celebrated postwar finance minister, said, investors have the memories of elephants, the hearts of lambs, and the legs of hares.

2. The second prerequisite for investment is stable macroeconomic policy. If real interest rates, real exchange rates, and inflation rates are violently unstable, time horizons inevitably shrink. There follows a decline in profitability and a reduced incentive to invest. Of course, real interest rates and real exchange rates are not the only variables that count. Even so, a comparison of Argentina and Chile is revealing. With the variability of its inflation and interest rates, it is little surprise that investment in Argentina has been low—negative in net terms—but also too short-horizon and too defensive from a social point of view. Interventionist policies, particularly the recurrent use of price controls and discretionary interference in firms' production and pricing plans, add to the instability of real exchange rates.

Investors abhor transitions. Unresolved issues stand in the way of investment, while continuity supports commitment. The sound rule in banking states, "Never lend in a transition." This rule applies with equal relevance to investment decisions. Governments therefore must make every effort to move quickly to a sustainable regime, and to put in place mechanisms that assure asset holders against abrupt moves. Governments must have a *policy*, not a day-to-day discretionary reaction to events. This idea is fundamental to what is called *Ordnungspolitik* in Germany—stability of rules. From 1948 onward this approach served Germany well.[1]

The critical missing link in many Latin American countries today is this stability of government policy. While Mexico exemplifies the advantage of purposeful government in fostering confidence, growth, and the return of flight capital, Argentina and Brazil show how the melting or the outright wrecking of economic institutions ultimately destroys the willingness of citizens to invest. The ensuing decapitalization undermines a country's ability to pay yesterday's wages. Standards of living decline and this makes politics increasingly difficult, because distribution rather than growth becomes the central issue. Workers call for expansion as the answer to their plight, but in fact the country's ability to sustain even past standards of living has been dissipated.

The key requirement for financial stability is a responsible budget. Anyone who invested in nominal assets in Argentina in the mid-1980s would today have in real terms less than 5 cents on the dollar. Even if people save, nobody can expect them to invest their savings in a financial system that robs them systematically. Much the same was true in the inflationary conditions of Yugoslavia and Poland before stabilization, and likewise in the Soviet Union. No surprise then that capital flight is endemic in an environment of protracted financial instability. In the area of finance the first priority must be the establishment of financial normality. The essential ingredients for this are budget balance and a stable exchange rate policy.

In nearly all countries most investment is financed from domestic savings (Feldstein and Horioka, 1980). When rules are stable, private saving is fostered. At the same time adequate tax receipts raise public saving, and public saving is as useful as private saving in fostering domestic investment.

3. The third requirement for effective investment is a proper system of financial intermediation. A key consideration is to achieve an intermediation system that focuses on lending to small and medium-sized firms for whom the agency costs of the capital market are prohibitive. Unfortunately banks do not find these businesses the most attractive, and rather favor large projects like LDC debt or vast real estate development projects. History is not on their side.

It is also crucial to create an institutional structure that makes it possible to have a broad equity market. Equity markets are essential to avoid an economy that is overindebted. Equity ownership may not offer the best means to achieve an efficient allocation of resources, but these problems fall far short of the risks of an overly leveraged economy.

External Finance as a Lever for Reform

It is easy to write down what is needed; the problem is to bring it about. Everybody accepts that investment has mainly to be financed by domestic savings. Even if things go really well, external finance will cover a small fraction of total investment—with a mixture of loans, purchase of existing capital, and investment in new capital.

At present the flow of private capital is extremely small. Everyone is waiting for everybody else. Like two Germans at the door, each says, "After you, please," judging it too risky to enter until someone else respectable has done so. This process will only end when political and economic stability seems likely.

So is there anything outsiders can do that will make a difference? They can do a lot. For economic reform is very difficult. For some years it involves large-scale unemployment and depressed standards of living. To sustain reform policies the government must have the maximum possible number of arguments to put to the people. One extremely convincing argument is that foreign aid is available only if the right policies are adhered to.

A major role of foreign aid has always been to secure good policies. Marshall Plan aid, which gave Western Europe 2 percent of its GNP per year from 1948 to 1951, was strongly conditioned on the adoption of market-oriented policies (DeLong and Eichengreen, 1991). And all IMF aid and the World Bank's Structural Adjustment Loans have had strong elements of conditionality. Indeed the IMF has established itself as the management consultant of the world, who can be blamed for all the bitter pills that the local chief executive hands out.

So the chief argument for foreign aid to the East is as the catalyst for the reform process—offering a blueprint around which a public that is torn by dissenting opinions and interests can organize its efforts. But this catalyst can only work if, when the conditions are met, real money flows.

Forms and Conditions of Aid

Two forms of money are critically needed. The first is a steady flow of balance of payments support. No Eastern European country can import enough to sustain reasonable economic activity without *either* running a current account deficit *or* devaluing to a level likely to produce riots and/or hyperinflation. Adequate support could determine whether Eastern Europe becomes a proper part of Europe or more akin to Latin America.

The second need is for a stock of standby foreign exchange to provide a cushion against economic shock and in particular to help stabilize the exchange rate. This is much less costly but very important. Other moneys can of course be provided with more specific ties—private sector loans, infrastructure support, and technical assistance. But the key financing needs are general balance of payments support and a stabilization fund. Given the debt position in the East, much of this money will have to be, like Marshall aid, in the form of grants.

To repeat, no aid should be provided under any of these headings except on strict conditions, above all full convertibility on current account. Foreign exchange should not be given to bureaucrats to allocate. Other conditions would include a rapid move to free all prices (except initially for housing, rents, energy, and utilities), tight budgets and tight credit, and an explicit plan for privatization.

Who Should Pay and How?

A key question is who should pay for this. The answer is, those who benefit. Western Europe will gain much more from this than the United States and Japan, in two ways. First, a flourishing East would buy most of its imports from Western Europe, thereby improving Western Europe's terms of trade. Second, if the East falters, it is Western Europe that will face the onrush of immigrants.

But not all Western Europe will gain from success in the East. The low-tech products of Spain, Portugal, Greece, Ireland, and to some extent the UK will suffer from Eastern competition, while the East imports machinery from the more advanced nations. Similarly, migrants would mostly flood into the more advanced nations, because they are richer and (mostly) nearer to the East. And Germany has one further special concern—the remaining Soviet soldiers on its soil.

So there is a delicate political game to be played. Coordination is essential because aid by one country affects the benefits accruing to all. Thus the European Community has to play a major role.

But the ultimate arbiter of respectability has to be the IMF, due to its responsibility for the international monetary order and its long experience of advice. This means that the United States has to be convinced. One function of this book could be to help in that process.

The United States has a major interest in stability in the East. There are still thousands of nuclear warheads in the Soviet area, aimed at the United States. Any wobble there would lead to more extra military expenditure in the United States than any conceivable aid program could cost. A major aid program to the republics along the lines of the "grand bargain" would cost the West under 5 percent of its annual defense budget.[2]

If the case for aid is clear, the next question is how to finance it. If it were done by borrowing, this would raise world real interest rates. Collins and Rodrik (1991) estimate that such a flow of $30 billion extra a year to the East would raise world real interest rates by around 1 percent. This would be a mistake. Aid to the East should be tax-financed. A major organizer of finance could be the European Commission and an obvious source for the extra money would be a cut in agricultural subsidies.

Consolidating the Debt

We have not so far considered the debt. As table 9 shows, most Eastern countries have a major burden of debt, and some of them make major resource transfers to the West in debt service. Would it not be more sensible to eliminate the debt, rather than supply new money as aid?

The question is a fair one, but misconceived. As we have said, a major purpose of aid is to acquire political leverage. Most Eastern countries (and certainly their citizens) feel that debt service is unfair. So a government telling its people that

Table 9
Debt and interest payments of Eastern European countries, 1990

Country	Debt as percent of exports	Interest payments as percent of exports
Poland	340	26
Hungary	267	19
Czechoslovakia	80	3
Bulgaria	327	21
Romania	18	—
USSR	111	9
Total	160	12

Source: UN Economic Commission for Europe, *Economic Survey of Europe*, 1990–1991.
Notes: Debt and interest payments are measured net. Poland's debt figure is before the negotiated debt reduction. Soviet exports are measured as exports to market economies only.

austerity will buy debt reduction would strike few chords. Nothing can replace the music of new money.

Moreover, the sanctity of contracts is an important principle of capitalism, and one that the Soviet Union at least upheld. So the obvious approach to debt is to consolidate it rather than write it off. All debt should become long-term. It should also be indexed, and pay a low real interest. This will reduce the main immediate burden of resource transfer, without destroying the balance sheets and confidence of lenders.

It is in the interest of East and West to work together to generate prosperity in the East. The West has all the cards, as the United States had in 1948. Let us hope it plays them as well.

Appendix 1

Economics of Migration: Further Evidence

We do not aim in this book to survey all the literature on migration. The state of knowledge up to the mid 1980s is well surveyed in Greenwood (1985, on the causes of internal migration) and in Greenwood and McDowell (1986, on the effects of international migration). Major recent studies are in Abowd and Freeman (1991) and in Borjas and Freeman (1992).

In general, the better earlier studies not quoted in the text support our main points. On the causes of internal migration, Mincer (1978) shows the effect of family ties in discouraging migration, and Graves and Linneman (1979) confirm the point that single people are more likely to move than people who are married. People are also more likely to move if they are educated (Sandell, 1977).

Unemployed people are more likely to move than others (da Vanzo, 1978, 1983), but (having moved) are more likely than others to return. Most but not all studies find that the ambient unemployment rate also affects migration. For Italy, Salvatore (1977) finds a strong influence of unemployment rates, and, like many others, he finds that the elasticity of migration with

respect to differences in job chances exceeds that with respect
to earnings differences. Most writers agree that, for given
unemployment differentials, a high general level of unemployment reduces migration (Ogilvy, 1982; Ledent, 1983).

There is some disagreement about the speed of migration
responses. Stark and Bloom (1985) stress the need for time for
channels of information to develop. Other writers such as
Drettakis (1976) have found rather short lags.

Turning to international migration, Pope and Withers (1990)
confirm the strong influence of Australian unemployment
upon immigration into Australia. Earlier, Thomas (1954, 1961)
showed clearly how European migration to America in the
nineteenth century proceeded in waves, peaking when
America was in boom and Europe in slump. He also showed
that the waves of labor migration coincided with waves of
capital flow, so that the resident population of America was
largely unharmed.

Other evidence on the effects of international migration comes
from Grossman (1982). She stresses that capital is particularly
complementary with immigrant labor, so that capitalists gain
especially from immigration, and (due to their segmented
position) existing immigrant workers lose. Native labor may
be relatively unaffected.

The fiscal effects of immigration are a matter of controversy,
and must differ from place to place. For the United States,
Simon (1987) stresses the low use of public services by immigrant families.

Employment effects are perhaps the largest issue of all. This has been a major subject of recent controversy in Australia (see for example the Bureau of Immigration Research conference of November 1990). Econometric evidence tends to show no clear effects of migration upon unemployment in Australia (Pope and Withers, 1990).

Appendix 2

Can Emigration Hurt
the Home Country?

In chapter 3 we presented the standard analysis of the economic effects of migration, in which there is taken to be a downward-sloping demand for labor in each country. Because of this downward-sloping demand, migration raises not only the incomes of the migrants themselves but also those of the similar workers left behind, while driving down the income of competing workers in the host nation. This implies in turn that migration is self-limiting: as labor becomes more abundant in the host nation and scarcer at home, the incentive to migrate diminishes.

The standard view, however, presumes that there are diminishing returns to labor in each nation. It is important at least to be aware of the contrary possibility that because of market size effects there will be increasing returns to labor in the host country, and that the labor demand curve may actually be upward-sloping. This may mean that out-migration lowers, instead of raising, the wages of workers left behind; in the worst-case scenario, emigration to the already prosperous European core could set in motion a vicious circle of declining incomes that transforms Eastern Europe into an impoverished area like Italy's Mezzogiorno or America's Appalachia.

In this appendix we sketch out a simple model of the role of increasing returns that helps suggest the conditions under which such a vicious circle might develop. This model focuses on the possible adverse effect of a reduction in the size of the domestic market for final goods. We should note, however, that similarly adverse effects might occur for several other reasons, notably a fall in the size of the pool of skilled labor or in the ability of the domestic market to support specialized suppliers of intermediate goods.

To focus on the issue, we imagine an economy in which labor is the only factor of production. This labor can be used to produce either exportables or import-competing goods. Sales of exportables depend on their price relative to competing goods produced elsewhere. Import-competing goods have some natural protection due to transportation costs; but they are subject to economies of scale, and thus cannot be produced competitively unless the domestic market is large enough. We also abstract from balance of payments issues, supposing that the economy spends all of its income.

Thus we can begin with a statement of a national income accounting identity:

$$Y = X + \sigma E$$

where Y is national income (measured in ecu), X is the value of exports, E is total national expenditure, and σ is the share of domestic expenditure that falls on domestically produced goods. We suppose that exports depend negatively on the wage rate (also measured in ecu):

$$X = X(w).$$

And we assume that all income is spent, so that

$E = Y.$

The share of domestic expenditure that falls on domestic goods (σ) depends on which goods are produced domestically. For a given wage rate, the range of goods that it is profitable to produce domestically depends on the size of the domestic market: the larger that market, the more goods can be produced domestically for less than the cost of imports. A rise in the wage rate, on the other hand, will make it less profitable to produce goods, and will normally lower σ. So we can write the share of spending on home goods as

$\sigma = \sigma(\underset{-}{w}, \underset{+}{E}).$

Employment takes place in both the export and import-competing sectors. Since labor is the only factor of production, if we ignore the possibility of monopoly profits we have

$D_L = Y/w$

for labor demand.

To analyze this model, we proceed in two steps. First we look at the determinants of output and employment holding the wage rate fixed; then we examine how these change with w to derive the labor demand curve.

Figure 11 shows the determination of national income (measured in units of domestic labor) for a given wage rate. The line DD shows how income depends on expenditure. But in equilibrium income equals expenditure, so that equilibrium is at point 1, where DD crosses the 45-degree line. As drawn, DD is steeper than the 45-degree line, which will be the case

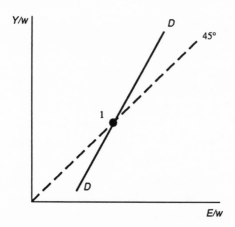

Figure 11
The equilibrium demand for labor, for given w.

only if (a) the limited size of the domestic market is a significant constraint on the range of goods produced domestically
and (b) an expansion of national income will substantially
relax that constraint. Algebraically, we have

$$d(Y/w)/d(E/w) = \sigma + (E/w)[d\sigma/d(E/w)].$$

If the limited size of the domestic market is a significant
constraint on the range of goods produced at home, the right
hand side can be bigger than unity, which is the case illustrated in the figure.

Now consider the effect of an increase in the wage rate. This
will reduce income for any given level of expenditure, for two
reasons. It will reduce exports, and it will make the range of
goods that can profitably be produced domestically smaller.
Thus DD will shift down. As shown in figure 12, however,
where the effect of a wage rise is illustrated by the shift from

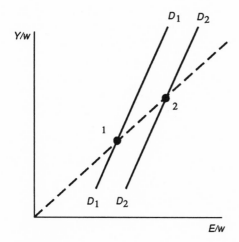

Figure 12
The equilibrium demand for labor rises when w falls.

D_1 to D_2, the equilibrium level of income and employment consistent with this wage rise actually increases.

The interpretation of this result is that the demand for labor D_L, shown in figure 12, is upward sloping. This is best understood by thinking of the wage rate as a function of the labor force rather than the other way around: the larger is the domestic labor force, the larger the domestic market, and hence the higher the wage rate that can be offered.

In figure 13 we also show labor supply curves S_1 and S_2. Emigration can be interpreted as a leftward shift of the domestic labor supply. Whenever the labor demand curve is upward-sloping, emigration will actually reduce the real wage of those who stay behind.

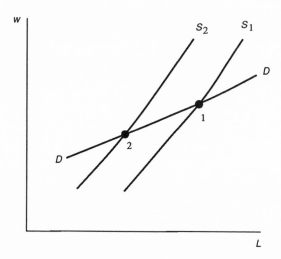

Figure 13
Emigration reduces w.

If emigration is itself strongly responsive to the domestic wage rate, this can lead to a vicious circle of economic contraction, which ends only when the economy has either shed all those workers willing to leave or shed all sectors whose profitability depends on the size of the domestic market. This is the nightmare scenario in which Eastern European nations are peripheralized, left with only those industries tied to immobile resources and those workers without the initiative to seek a better life. Given both the natural barriers of differences in language and culture and the legal barriers, emigration from Eastern Europe is unlikely to reach the proportions necessary for such a scenario. While a vicious circle of contraction seems unlikely, however, the suggestion that emigration may actually reduce the real wages of those who stay at home is by no means unreasonable.

Notes

1 Overview

1. Prices are of course somewhat higher in Germany, but if he sends the money home the Polish worker has precisely multiplied his zloty income by 10.

2. We use the term Eastern Europe to include Poland, Hungary, Czechoslovakia, Bulgaria, Romania, Yugoslavia, and the European parts of the former USSR.

3. On the Mexican case, see Commission for the Study of International Migration and Cooperative Economic Development (1990) and Dornbusch (1991).

4. Half of these Germans are in the Soviet area. Some estimates of the number of Germans in that area are higher than those quoted here. The definition of an ethnic German is extremely wide and does not require a relative to have been born in Germany. Many ethnic Germans are descended from the Germans who were encouraged to go east in previous centuries by Catherine the Great and other rulers as bearers of know-how.

5. Chesnais (1991). Under the recent agreement between Russia and Germany, many of the ethnic Germans who were deported eastward by Stalin in 1941 will be resettled near the Volga. This will help to reduce the emigration of Germans from Russia.

6. Maillat (1987), p. 59 (1981 data); OECD (1985).

2 Migration: The Pressure to Move

1. Akerlof et al. (1991), table 9; Hönekopp (1991).

2. Another group that may exercise a legal right of entry to Germany is the Gypsies. There are 2.5–4 million Gypsies in Eastern Europe and, as a result of Nazi persecution, they could seek entry to Germany under the right to reparation.

3. *Voprovy Economiki*, no. 7, 1991. The proportions were very similar in all educational groups, but higher for people under 40 than for older people.

4. This is a somewhat loose statement, since the relative populations are affected by continent-specific birth and death rates and not only by net migration.

5. The number was 0.8 million in 1970 and 4.0 million in 1988 (Vernez and Ronfeldt, 1991).

6. Chesnais (1991), p. 9.

7. Cross-section analyses are more feasible. In the United States in the late 1960s controls were similar for all foreign scientists, and Psacharopoulos showed that the fraction of scientists from each country draining to the United States was inversely related to the source country's income per capita (Bhagwati, 1976).

8. For a survey see Greenwood (1985).

9. Other variables were average heating degree-days, population density, regional dummies, share of agriculture, and sectoral composition.

10. Layard et al. (1991), chapter 6.

11. Based on Layard et al. (1991), chapter 6. Comparable figures for Spain are $0.025/u$ percent for the effect of a 10 percent lower wage, and $0.09/u$ percent for the effect of a 10 percent lower employment rate, where u is the national unemployment rate. See Bentolila and Dolado (1991), pp. 212–213.

12. See Pissarides and Wadsworth (1989).

13. They also claimed to show the unimportance of wages, but their argument at this point is unconvincing.

14. Poland began issuing passports reasonably freely in 1985.

15. In a simple infection model the proportion of the uninfected population becoming infected per period is proportional to the number already infected. Thus, if p is the proportion of the total population infected so far,

$$\dot{p}/(1-p) = \alpha p.$$

16. If actual migration is held below the desired level, this raises the subsequent demand to migrate on stock adjustment grounds and reduces the demand to migrate on infection grounds.

17. Simon (1987). By the mid-1980s the flow was down to 200,000 a year.

18. Residence permits in the Schengen area will presumably be allocated on a European-wide basis.

19. Mexicans can of course enter the United States as tourists if they have the necessary documents.

20. For employers caught for the first time, the fine is currently between $250 and $2,000 per illegal worker. For repeated offenders, this can rise to $3,000 plus 6 months in prison.

21. As Walter (1991) points out, it has been very unsatisfactory that the German government should give maintenance allowances to asylum seekers pending their hearing (often for a long period), while not allowing them to earn a livelihood.

3 Migration: The Likely Effects

1. In this formulation K means effective capital, after allowing for any differences between East and West in the degree of technical progress. Then

$$\frac{W_E}{W_W} = \left(\frac{K_E}{K_W}\right)^{\frac{1}{4}} \left(\frac{L_W}{L_E}\right)^{\frac{1}{4}}.$$

If we wish to raise W_E/W_W by a multiple 3.3 we have to raise L_W/L_E by a multiple $(3.3)^4$. The calculation also implies that at present, with $W_E/W_W = 0.1$, $K_E/K_W \cong (0.1)^4$. This seems rather extreme.

2. Borjas (1990) has shown that the skill mix of migrants is clearly sensitive to the wage structure in the sending country.

3. One argument in favor of skilled migration that we reject is the main one used by Borjas (1990), that it would raise average productivity in the receiving country (relative to unskilled migration). It is difficult to think of any reason why average productivity (averaged over different people) should be of any significance.

4. See Layard et al. (1991), chapter 6.

5. Layard et al. (1991), chapter 5. A different issue is the steady-state unemployment rates for immigrants and others. When immigrants have language difficulties, their rates will inevitably be higher than for natives.

6. The boatlift of some 125,000 Cubans from Mariel to Miami in mid-1980 seemed to offer a perfect controlled experiment. On a before-and-after basis there was no effect on native wages or employment rates (Card, 1990). But this seems to be due to the fact that the Miami population growth rate fell sharply in the 1980s:

Growth rate of population (percent per annum)

	Pre-1980	Post-1980
Miami	2.5	1.4
Rest of Florida	3.9	3.4

7. Many studies have simply regressed Δw on Δp, where w is native wages and p is the immigrant proportion of the population, using OLS. But there is clearly the danger that immigration and wages are both affected by local demand factors. Only if p is instrumented can we find the effect of the exogenous component of it upon w. The result we quote from Altonji and Card is the instrumented result. Butcher and Card (1991) quote uninstrumented results from the 1980s. In that period the movement of natives did not affect the movement of immigrants (presumably because immigrants followed demand more than before), and it is not surprising that Δw and Δp are not then negatively correlated.

8. The regression is

$$\log\left(\frac{W_L}{W_M}\right) = \underset{(0.138)}{-0.322} \log\left(\frac{N_L}{N_M}\right) + 0.023 \, \text{Time} + \text{const.}$$

estimated on the years 1963–1987, where L denotes less educated (high school not completed) and M denotes more educated. Notice that this assumes separability between labor types and capital, which for historical analysis is probably all right in a period when the overall capital/labor ratio was roughly constant.

4 Free Trade with the West

1. $(0.7 - 0.3)20\% = 8\%$.

5 Aid and Capital Flows

1. Giersch et al. (1991).

2. For more on this and other arguments of US self-interest see Allison and Yavlinsky (1991). As Collins and Rodrik (1991) point out, debt-financed aid to the East could raise world real interest rates, which would hurt the United States (as a debtor) and benefit Japan (as a creditor). But see our proposal below for tax finance.

References

Abowd, J. M., and R. B. Freeman (eds.). 1991. *Immigration, Trade, and the Labor Market*. National Bureau of Economic Research, University of Chicago Press.

Akerlof, G., A. Rose, J. Yellen, and H. Hessenius. 1991. "East Germany in from the Cold: The Economic Aftermath of Currency Union." Conference of the Brookings Panel on Economic Activity, Washington, D.C., vol. 1.

Allison, G., and G. Yavlinsky. 1991. "Window of Opportunity: Joint Program for Western Co-operation in the Soviet Transformation to Democracy and the Market Economy." Harvard and EPCenter USSR, mimeo.

Altonji, J., and D. Card. 1991. "The Effects of Immigration on the Labor Market Outcomes of Less-Skilled Natives." In Abowd and Freeman (1991).

Attanasio, O., and F. Padoa-Schioppa. 1991. "Regional Inequalities, Migration and Mismatch in Italy, 1960–86." In Padoa-Schioppa (1991), 237–324.

Barro, R., and X. Sala-i-Martin. 1991. "Convergence across States and Regions." Unpublished manuscript, Harvard University.

Bentolila, S., and J. Dolado. 1991. "Mismatch and Internal Migration in Spain, 1962–86." In Padoa-Schioppa (1991), 182–236.

Bhagwati, J. 1976. "The International Brain Drain and Taxation." In J. Bhagwati (ed.), *The Brain Drain and Taxation II, Theory and Empirical Analysis*. North Holland.

Blackhurst, R. 1991. "Implications of the Changes in Eastern Europe for the World Economy." *The Transformation of Socialist Economies*, Kiel Institute of World Economics, Conference, 26–28 June.

Blanchard, O., and R. Layard. 1990. "Economic Change in Poland." *The Polish Transformation: Programme and Progress*. Centre for Research into Communist Economies, London.

Blanchard, O., and R. Layard. 1991. "How to Privatise." Centre for Economic Performance, London School of Economics, mimeo.

Blanchard, O., and L. Summers. 1986. "Hysteresis and the European Unemployment Problem." In S. Fischer (ed.), *NBER Macroeconomics Annual 1986*. MIT Press.

Borjas, G. 1990. *Friends or Strangers: The Impact of Immigrants on the US Economy*. Basic Books.

Borjas, G., and R. Freeman (eds.). 1992. *The Determinants and Effects of Immigration on the U.S. and Source Economies*. Forthcoming.

Borjas, G., R. Freeman, and L. Katz. 1992. "On the Labor Market Effects of Immigration and Trade." In Borjas and Freeman (1992).

Butcher, K. F., and D. Card. 1991. "Immigration and Wages, Evidence from the 1980s." *American Economic Review*, 81, no. 2 (May), 292–296.

Calvaruso, C. 1987. "Illegal Immigration to Italy." In OECD (1987), 306–314.

Card, D. 1990. "The Impact of the Mariel Boatlift on the Miami Labour Market." *Industrial and Labor Relations Review*, 43, no. 2 (January), 245–257.

Chesnais, J.-C. 1991. "Migration from Eastern to Western Europe, Past (1946–1989) and Future (1990–2000)." Paper presented to the Conference of Ministers on the Movement of Persons Coming from Central and Eastern European Countries, Council of Europe.

Coleman, D. 1990. "Contrasting Age-Structures of East and Western Europe and the Soviet Union: Demographic Curiosity or Useful Resource?" From the International Symposium on Demographic Processes in the USSR in the 20th Century in the Context of the European Experience, Tbilisi.

Collins, S., and D. Rodrik. 1991. "Eastern Europe and the Soviet Union in the World Economy." Institute for International Economics, Washington, D.C.

Commission for the Study of International Migration and Cooperative Economic Development, 1990. *Unauthorized Migration: An Economic Development Response*. Washington, D.C. July.

Da Vanzo, J. 1978. "Does Unemployment Affect Migration? Evidence from Micro Data." *Review of Economics and Statistics*, 60, 504–514.

Da Vanzo, J. 1983. "Repeat Migration in the United States: Who Moves Back and Who Moves On?" *Review of Economics and Statistics*, 65, 552–559.

DeLong, J. B., and B. Eichengreen. 1991. "The Marshall Plan: History's Most Successful Structural Adjustment Program." Harvard University and University of California, Berkeley, mimeo.

Dornbusch, R. 1991. "US-Mexico Free Trade: Good Jobs at Good Wages." Testimony before the Subcommittee on Labor-Management Relations and Employment Opportunities, Committee on Education and Labor, U.S. House of Representatives.

Drettakis, F. G. 1976. "Distributed Lag Models for the Quarterly Migration Flows of West Germany, 1962–72." *Journal of the Royal Statistical Society*, 139, 365–373.

Feldstein, M. S., and C. Horioka. 1980. "Domestic Saving and International Capital Flows." *The Economic Journal*, no. 90 (June), 314–329.

Filer, R. 1992. "The Impact of Immigrant Arrivals on Migratory Patterns of Native Workers." In Borjas and Freeman (1992).

Giersch, H., K.-H. Paqué, and H. Schmieding. 1991. "The Fading Miracle: Forty Years of Economic Policy in West Germany." Mimeo; forthcoming from Cambridge University Press.

Graves, P., and P. Linneman. 1979. "Household Migration: Theoretical and Empirical Results." *Journal of Urban Economics*, 6, 383–404.

Greenwood, M. 1985. "Human Migration: Theory, Models and Empirical Studies." *Journal of Regional Sciences*, 25, 521–544.

Greenwood, M., and J. McDowell. 1986. "The Factor Market Consequences of U.S. Immigration." *Journal of Economic Literature*, 24, 1738–1772.

Grossman, J. B. 1982. "The Substitutability of Natives and Immigrants in Production." *Review of Economics and Statistics*, 64, no. 4, 596–603.

Hansen, B. 1991. "Europe's Shocking Immigration Policies." University of California, Berkeley, mimeo.

Harris, J., and M. Todaro. 1970. "Migration, Unemployment and Development: A Two-Sector Analysis." *American Economic Review*, 60, no. 1, 126–142.

Hönekopp, E. 1991. "Migratory Movements from Countries of Central and Eastern Europe: Causes and Characteristics, Present Situation and Possible Future Trends—the Cases of Germany and Austria." Paper presented to the Conference of Ministers on the Movement of Persons Coming from Central and Eastern European Countries, Council of Europe.

Hunt, J. 1991. "The Impact of the 1962 Repatriates from Algeria on the French Labour Market." Unpublished manuscript, Harvard University.

Kindleberger, C. 1967. *Europe's Post-War Growth*. Harvard University Press.

Krugman, P. 1991. *Geography and Trade*. MIT Press.

Krugman, P., and J. Bhagwati. 1976. "The Decision to Migrate: A Survey." In J. Bhagwati (ed.), *The Brain Drain and Taxation II, Theory and Empirical Analysis*. North Holland.

Layard, R., S. Nickell, and R. Jackman. 1991. *Unemployment: Macroeconomic Performance and the Labour Market*. Oxford University Press.

Ledent, J. 1983. "Demoeconomic Modelling of Interprovincial Migration in Canada: The Longitudinal Case." Paper presented at the 23rd European Congress of the Regional Science Association, France.

Maillat, D. 1987. "European Receiving Countries." In OECD (1987), 38–63.

Mincer, J. 1978. "Family Migration Decisions." *Journal of Political Economy*, 86, 749–773.

OECD, 1985. "The Labour Market Implications of International Migration in Selected OECD countries." Chapter III in *Employment Outlook*, September.

OECD, 1987. *The Future of Migration.*

Ogilvy, A. A. 1982. "Population Migration between the Regions of Great Britain, 1971–79." *Regional Studies*, 16, 65–73.

Padoa-Schioppa, F. (ed.). 1991. *Mismatch and Labour Mobility.* Cambridge University Press.

Piore, M. 1979. *Birds of Passage.* Cambridge University Press.

Pissarides, C., and J. Wadsworth. 1989. "Unemployment and the Inter-Regional Mobility of Labour." *Economic Journal*, 99, 739–755.

Pope, D., and G. Withers. 1990. "Do Migrants Rob Jobs from Locals? Lessons of Australian History." Working Papers in Economic History, no. 133.

Salvatore, D. 1977. "An Econometric Analysis of Internal Migration in Italy." *Journal of Regional Science*, 17, 395–408.

Sandell, S. 1977. "Women and the Economics of Family Migration." *Review of Economics and Statistics*, 59, 406–414.

Simon, G. 1987. "Migration in Southern Europe: An Overview." In OECD (1987), 258–291.

Simon, J. L. 1984. "Immigrants, Taxes, and Welfare in the United States." *Population and Development Review*, 10, no. 1, 55–69.

Smith, S. 1986. *Britain's Shadow Economy.* Oxford University Press.

Stark, O., and D. Bloom. 1985. "The New Economics of Labor Migration." *American Economic Review*, 75, 173–178.

Thomas, B. 1954. *Migration and Economic Growth.* Cambridge University Press.

Thomas, B. 1961. *International Migration and Economic Development.* Unesco.

Thomas, B. 1972. *Migration and Urban Development.* Methuen.

Vernez, G., and D. Ronfeldt. 1991. "The Current Situation in Mexican Immigration." *Science*, 251 (March), 1189–1193.

Walter, N. 1991. "Immigration—Policy Options for Europe." Paper presented to the Bertelsmann Stiftung Working Group on "Europe's Role in World Affairs," Budapest, June 14–15.

Withers, G., and D. Pope. 1985. "Immigration and Unemployment." *Economic Record*, 61 (173), 554–563.